THE BOOK OF ANSWERS

Trusting your inner Oracle

GAIA ELLIOT

The world is a mysterious and uncertain place. But even in the face of challenge and discomfort, we have the opportunity to develop our strengths and talents. Often, we feel uneasy about the way ahead and it's not clear to us how we can manifest our true desires. In these moments, we need to look to the innate wisdom we share with the universe and trust it. The answers we seek aren't always obvious or easy to recognise, as we are not always looking in the right place. Sometimes we just have to put one foot in front of the other until the answer reveals itself; sometimes it comes to us in a waking dream, creative spark or connection, and the planets suddenly appear to align.

Whatever your life's path, you have more power than you realise and the answers you seek are closer than you think. The universe is a resource and its wisdom is available to you through the natural world, your relationship with yourself and with other people, and your overall attitude to all of these. Making your mindset positive, and actively seeking what is available to you, is key and this requires some focus and application. When this approach becomes a way of being, then you know you are maximising life's opportunities. Believing this is the first step; realising it through the use of *The Book of Answers* is the second.

HOW TO USE THIS BOOK

Think of this book as an inner resource that provides you with the insights you need to make your decisions. Hold the book in your dominant hand and focus on the power of the universe, imagining it as available to you *in this moment* while you gather your thoughts and concentrate on your question. Your question may be no more than a fleeting query about some issue at work, or it may be a major dilemma or a difficult decision you need to make. No matter. Even if the answer isn't immediately obvious, have faith and be open to the myriad ways the relevant answer might reveal itself.

That is the power you have available to you, to manifest the next step in your daily life, your career or your relationships.

Bear in mind that time is a construct we impose on our lives, necessary to schedule a meeting or catch a train. But in reality, it is not always obvious that something will change in an hour, a day, a week or a year. Sometimes we have lessons to learn before things clarify, so *trust the process* and it will become clear, in time, that time is your friend.

Take a moment to be alert to the beauty of the natural world: the whorl of a snail's shell, the flight of a feather, the texture of a pebble, the fall of a wave. Each has its own harmony to help rebalance yours.

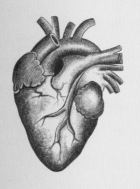

You are the author
of your own future; start
writing it with compassion
and positivity.

If you are feeling
overwhelmed, press pause
and focus on your breathing.
In for a count of five, hold for
a count of five, out for a
count of five. Practise this
daily and it becomes an
emergency resource.

Every sunset is a new dawn somewhere in the world. Cherish the daily renewal of life and respect its rhythms; your body and soul will thank you for it.

Do not make the past
a life sentence. Learn its
lessons and move on.

Stay curious about people, places and experiences. Curiosity enhances life and sparks creativity and connections.

Ripeness is all. Allow the
universe to guide you and
practice patience until you
are ready.

When your inner child
wants to dance, turn the
music up loud and ask
others to join you.

Happiness isn't
an end result.
It's a daily practice
of recognising and
building on those
small moments that
enhance our lives.

When in doubt, walk. Walking enables creativity and promotes calm. It helps access the unconscious brain, in which so many answers are stored.

Say 'yes' not because
you feel you ought to,
but because it feels right
to you.

Growing old
is a privilege. Learn
from the process and
don't resent the
passing of the years.

Dissatisfaction can
be a spur to greater
endeavour, don't
disregard it.

Sometimes the
simplest things can
refresh your soul:
the dawn chorus,
a cup of tea made
for you by a friend,
a new moon.

Treat obstacles
as stepping stones
to a better future.

Living with uncertainty
is often difficult but
necessary: be patient
with the world, it moves
at its own pace.

You are not defined by
what happens to you,
but how you use the
opportunity to grow.

The value of rest and
relaxation is often
underrated and will help
you retain focus
in a busy world.

Boredom is your friend.
It allows time to wonder
at the world and frees
the mind to make
connections.

Smile more.
This activates the
feel-good centre in your
brain as well as inviting
a positive response from
those around you.

Every destination
requires a journey,
so be sure to enjoy
the ride.

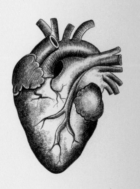

Remember to let
go of ideas that
no longer serve you.
If you find this difficult,
write them down
on a piece of paper, leave
overnight, then burn
outdoors and allow the
ashes to fly away.

This too shall pass.

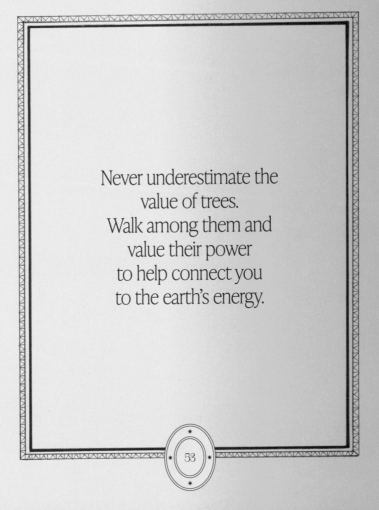

Never underestimate the
value of trees.
Walk among them and
value their power
to help connect you
to the earth's energy.

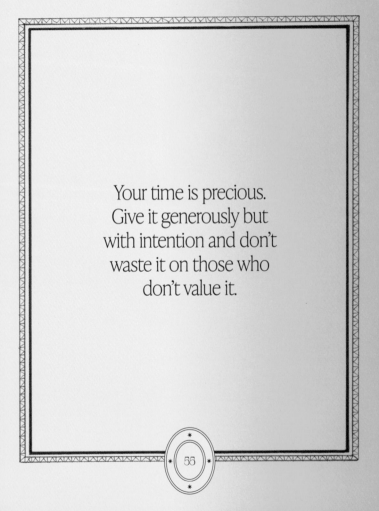

Your time is precious.
Give it generously but
with intention and don't
waste it on those who
don't value it.

Just keep going.
No feeling is final.

We are what we
repeatedly do. Make
your everyday habits
positive and make the
positive a habit.

When in doubt, press
pause and sleep on it.

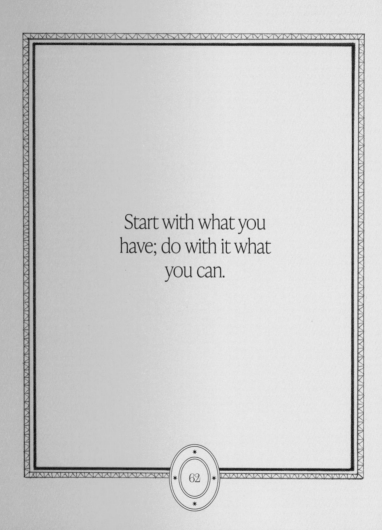

Start with what you have; do with it what you can.

A 'mistake' is just
something you did that
didn't get you the result
you wanted.

Value the benefit of the 'second wind'. When you feel physically overwhelmed or that you've lost your way, press pause and trust your inner resources to revitalise you.

Love isn't finite.
It's an act of endless
forgiveness that frees
you from your past.

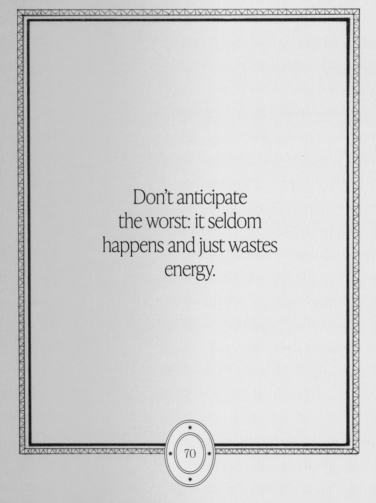

Don't anticipate
the worst: it seldom
happens and just wastes
energy.

UTILISE YOUR SENSES
TO RECONNECT
WITH THE WORLD

1

Watch a bee pollinating a flower.

2

Listen to the rainfall nourishing the earth.

3

Feel the texture of the fabric
as you fold your bed linen.

4

Glory in the aroma of a lily.

5

Savour the taste of an apple.

Your greatest investment
is always in yourself.

Paying it forwards doesn't
mean neglecting your own
needs; it just answers
them in unexpected ways.

Wishing on a star gives
you a moment
to refocus and re-ignite
that dream.

When nothing seems to
work, don't try harder.
Do something different.

The rainbow is better
than the pot of gold
at its end, because the
rainbow is here now and
the pot of gold never
turns out quite as you
expected.

Walk through a difficult
task in your mind until it
feels familiar.

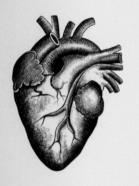

As much as you want to
be heard, also take the
time to listen.

Life is a series
of choices: choose
wisely what you
accept and decline.

Your birthday is the
beginning of your
personal new year
and always a cause
for celebration.

Slow down. Shifting into
a lower gear gives you
more purchase on the
road ahead and often
yields better results.

Find three different ways
to say 'yes' today.

Resilience can only be
learnt through adversity;
only through experience
is it possible to learn how
to manage difficult times.

Keep a journal and handwrite your thoughts and intentions. The hand-eye connection helps you to focus and formulate new creative ideas.

Never let the sun go
down on an argument:
make your peace before
you sleep.

It's not what happens
to you that counts, but
what you do with it.

Courage comes from
the French word
for the heart: *cœur*.

When the going gets tough, the tough take heart.

Don't allow procrastination
to stop you from getting
started: the best time
to start is now.

GREEN VISTAS
REFRESH NEURAL
ACTIVITY

1

Go for a walk among nature
to feel it in action.

2

Surround yourself with houseplants.

3

Spend 10 minutes gardening,
even if you're only planting up
a window box.

4

Make your screensaver a beautiful,
natural view of the countryside.
Even a picture of a rural scene on the
wall can refresh your brain.

Choosing to do nothing
is still a choice.

Water is soothing.
Metaphorically wash away
your troubles every
morning or evening when
you shower or bathe.

Make overwhelming
tasks feel manageable
by working in ten-minute
blocks until you've
completed an hour's
work. Take a break and
start again.

Do not base your
personal happiness
on things over which
you have no control.

It's not the tools
you have available
to you that matter, but
what you do with them
to achieve your aims.

How successful you are
depends on three things:
how clear your plan
is, how hard you try and
how far your aim accords
with your values.

Time is a precious
commodity and when it
is given with love,
it blesses those who give
as well as those who
receive.

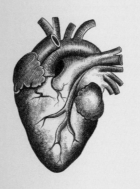

Sometimes, there are more than two sides to every story, but the only one on which you can act is your own.

If you have been happy
in the past, you will
be happy again.

Learn to distinguish
between setting
boundaries and saying
'no'. The first will keep
you on track, the second
may deny you an
opportunity.

Remember to differentiate
between your goals and
your dreams: goals are the
outcome that your
dreams can fuel.

Other people's expectations
of you are based on their
expectations of themselves,
and you can choose to live
up to these or not.

You can choose
between making the
worst of a difficult
situation, or the best.
By choosing to make
the worst you just stall;
by choosing to make
the best of things you
can progress.

Imagine and
visualise your best
self: now work out
how you got there.

If the way forward seems
dark, light a candle
in your mind. Focus
on its flame. Watch how
it stays steady even
in a draft. Be that flame.

Time is just a construct
we devised to help
us stay on schedule.

USE YOUR SENSES
TO RECONNECT
BODY AND MIND

1

Ground your energy by going barefoot.

2

Lift your mood by smelling a rose.

3

Soothe your skin with natural oils.

4

Listen to birdsong when you can.

5

Savour the food that you eat.
Each is its own blessing.

If you keep repeating
a pattern that is
unhelpful to you, you
will need to change
the pattern to one that
does the opposite.

Every day you make
around 30,000 decisions.
Mostly you do this
instinctively, using intuition
based on lived experience.
Trust your intuition and
become more decisive.

If the grass looks greener
on the other side, water
the grass on your side.

When all else seems
to be failing you,
take a leap of faith.

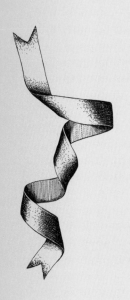

If you need to sleep
more serenely, infuse
some honey with a
handful of lemon balm
leaves and lavender,
then add to a glass
of warm milk to help
settle your mind.

Shake up your creative
energy by challenging your
senses. Wear the colour
red. Walk a different route
to work. Visit a gallery
on your lunch hour. Swap
your morning coffee for
a herbal tea.

Some days are just hard.
They help us appreciate
easier times.

If saving money isn't
your forte, think of it as
an investment in yourself.
However small the
amount, it will add
up over time.

Practise nurturing a place
of inner peace. You may
not need this resource
today, but when you
do it will be there.

Laughter shouldn't
be saved for special
occasions but shared
every day.

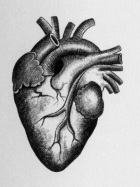

When someone gives you
the gift of their time, accept
it graciously; it may be all
they have to offer.

If being a problem means
doing what's right to
solve a problem, then
you're not a problem.

When in doubt, be kind.
If you are kind first to
yourself, then you will feel
kind towards others.

Connect your feelings
to rational thought
by taking a lesson from
the dragonfly, which lives
between the realms
of water and air.

Life can't be lived
in a vacuum, you need
to get out there and let
the universe reveal its
plan for you.

Love won't die if you
replenish its source. Take
a moment every day
to remember who and
what you love.

Your experience
of life is yours alone:
its opportunities can
be found wherever
you choose to look.

Reconnect body and mind by taking a freshly picked sprig of lemon balm, placing it in a freshly poured glass of water and leaving it in the sun for an hour before drinking.

Do not fear that
which you wish to do,
there is no failure
in attempting it.

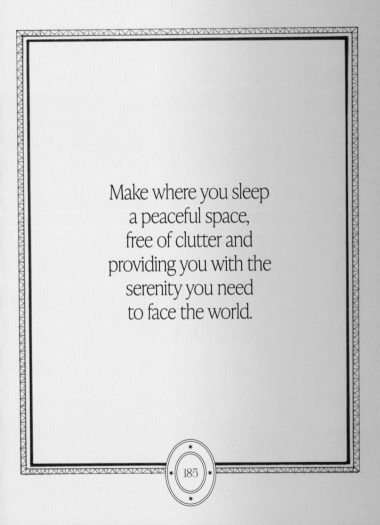

Make where you sleep
a peaceful space,
free of clutter and
providing you with the
serenity you need
to face the world.

If your to-do list seems
daunting, start with the easiest
task. It will give you the
confidence to tackle the next
item and the next,
until suddenly it's done.

EVERY NEW MOON
IS THE BEGINNING
OF A POWERFUL
NEW LUNAR CYCLE

USE IT TO MANIFEST
YOUR AIMS AND
DESIRES

1

Light a candle.

2

Hold your favourite crystal in your
left hand to connect its energy
to your heart.

3

Write down the three words that
best sum up what you want.

4

Place this under your pillow and
sleep on it to cement your intention.

Don't allow self-sacrifice
to lead to resentment.
Factor your own needs
into a group equation
to avoid this.

The answer to most
questions is a simple
'yes' or 'no'.

When in doubt,
remember the magic
of three: think it,
plan it, do it.

The key is a symbol
of unlocking. Focus
on this to unlock your
potential and the door
to a new path.

When you see a white feather,
imagine it comes from
an angel's wing, reminding
you that your spirit guide
is there for you.

Silence can be a balm
to the soul. Include
some in your life.

Do not underestimate the power in just showing up. Your presence has huge value.

You can travel in the
mind as well as the body.
Reading fiction will take
you to new worlds,
provide new insights and
offer new ideas about
how the world works.

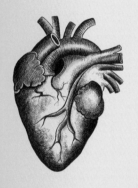

In an uncertain world,
learn to trust that
every day is a new
opportunity to make
a difference to your life.

Find out what motivates you
– is it a carrot or a stick? –
and use it to get started.

Don't waste your time living someone else's version of your life, live your own authentic dreams.

Live in rhythm with the universe and look to its signs to guide you.

When you know your own
worth, no one can make you
feel worthless.

Use your imagination
to unlock new
possibilities. Imagine
yourself in a positive
place and then work
out how to get there.

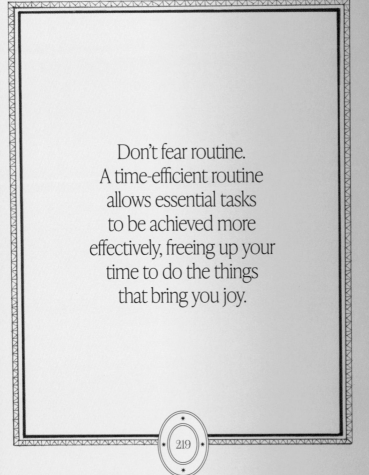

Don't fear routine.
A time-efficient routine
allows essential tasks
to be achieved more
effectively, freeing up your
time to do the things
that bring you joy.

Wear something red
to lift your mood and give
you courage.

When you get the chance, find a beautiful tree and lie underneath it to watch the patterns the leaves make on the sky. It will remind you of the gifts the universe has for you.

It's not how long it takes
to reach your destination
that matters, but what the
journey can teach you.

Remember that it can
take 10 years to become
an overnight sensation.
Start now.

Not everything is a puzzle
to be solved. Sometimes you
just need to wait for the facts
to reveal themselves.

When someone shows
you who they are,
believe them.

Learn something new.
Focusing hard on a new
skill or activity helps clear
your brain of clutter and
keeps your thoughts
creative and fresh.

If an old friend comes
into your mind
spontaneously and
unexpectedly, make
contact as they may
be thinking of you too.

Trust your gut when
it tells you to say 'no'.
Maintaining your
boundaries is healthy
and serves you better
in the long run.

A full moon is a time
for celebration. Use
its reflected light to
illuminate your progress
through the last lunar cycle.
Take a moment
to reflect on the certainty
of nature's rhythms
and work with them.

Remember that your
thoughts are based
on your beliefs and vice
versa. Make sure those
beliefs are accurate and
challenge them if they
no longer serve you.

When you give a hug you
automatically get one back.

Always make time
to celebrate your
achievements, your friends,
your life. Life is as good
as you choose to make it.

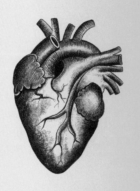

WHEN YOUR ENERGY IS DEPLETED, TAKE THESE THREE STEPS TO REPLENISH IT

1
Pause.

2
Breathe.

3
Focus.

You've got this.

Thinking negatively
is a survival tactic,
but it can impinge
on your daily activities.
Counteract these
thoughts by practising
gratitude.

Ten per cent of life is what
happens to you: the rest
is about how you respond.
What doesn't enhance
your life, doesn't belong
in your life.

Do something today that
you've never done before.
Paint a picture. Swim
in the sea in winter. Speak
to a stranger on the bus.
Challenge your norm and
see what transpires.

Spring always returns.
It's one of life's greatest
guarantees.

Everyone has the same
24 hours in the day, some
just use it more effectively.
You can too.

Practise self-compassion
and kindness to foster
resilience. It makes it easier
to feel positive about
others too.

If someone makes you feel
you're 'too much', they are not
your people.

262

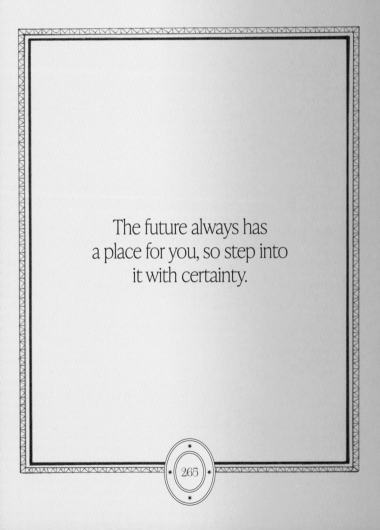

The future always has
a place for you, so step into
it with certainty.

If your plan isn't working out, shift the position from which you view your goal.

A cup of freshly brewed
mint tea will soothe your
stomach, your nerves
and your soul all at the
same time.

It takes time to see that
wishes can be fulfilled.

Sometimes you just need
to rest. Almost everything
works better after you
unplug for a while.

Don't forget, some
of your best ideas haven't
happened yet.

At the end of each day,
list three good things that
have happened to you.

In a world of uncertainty,
look to the cycles
of nature to ground you.

Don't dream about success,
work for it.

Better to be a first-rate
version of yourself than
a second-rate version
of someone else.

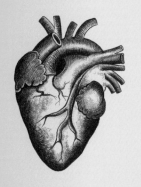

Change is always possible.
Start small and watch
it happen.

Daily self-care is essential
to survival.

Your boundaries define who you are, but do not let them remove you from positive opportunities. Sometimes they need to be re-assessed.

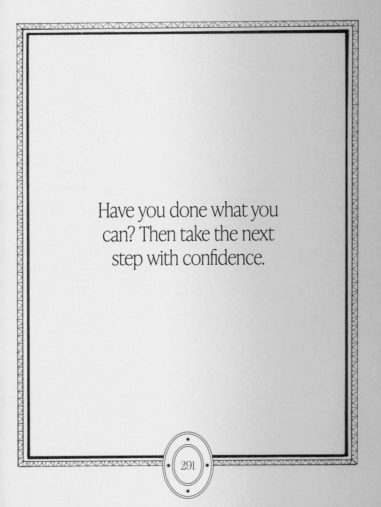

Have you done what you can? Then take the next step with confidence.

There's always time
to smell the roses.

When you lack inspiration,
take a clear quartz crystal
in your right hand, place your
left on top and connect the
two. Close your eyes, listen
to your heart and see what
comes up.

Taking risks is part of life.
Trust the process.

To develop your intuition,
make a note of fleeting
thoughts and ideas and
observe how these connect
with your external world.

In a circle of compassion,
you are at its centre.

Greet each new season
with joy. Spring to lift
your heart. Summer
to celebrate life. Autumn
to count your blessings.
Winter to recharge your
body and mind.

It's never too late to plan
a new beginning.

Foster resilience by remembering how you have successfully handled difficulties in the past. Keep this success in mind as you navigate new problems.

If you're looking
for a sign, this is it.

Start with what you
have and build
on its possibilities.

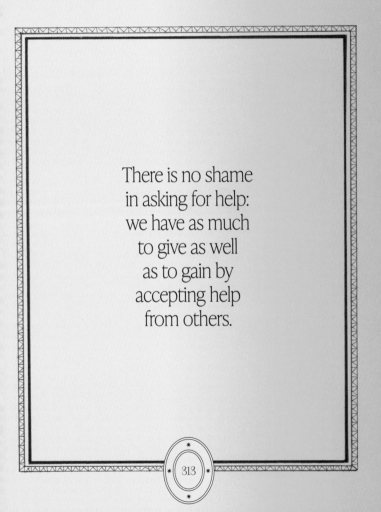

There is no shame
in asking for help:
we have as much
to give as well
as to gain by
accepting help
from others.

Confidence comes from
rising to a challenge,
not ignoring it.

Cleanse your workspace
by keeping a piece of clear
quartz on your desk.

The best is yet to come.

A smile is a gift to self
as well as to the recipient.
It's never wasted.

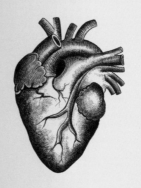

To cleanse your energy
and reinvigorate your
purpose, place a stem
of freshly picked rosemary
in a glass of freshly poured
water and leave in the
sunshine for an hour
before drinking.

Beware the barrenness
of a busy life.

To thrive in life is an active process and requires investment: keep your body strong and your mind curious.

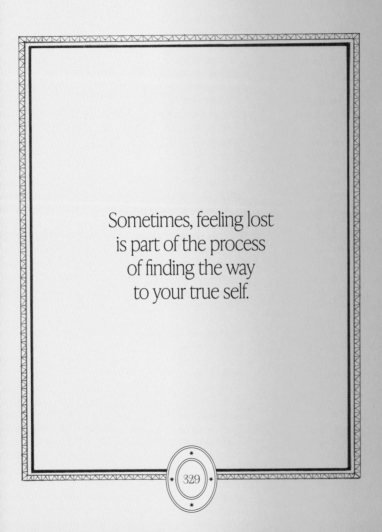

Sometimes, feeling lost
is part of the process
of finding the way
to your true self.

Make sure there is one
day of rest in your week.
To recharge and restore
the body and mind is an
important part of life.

Be open to your sensual
self's capacity to uplift your
soul. You have five senses for
a reason, so enjoy the world
they open up to you.

Sometimes you just
have to say 'no'.

Every journey has to start with an intention and that's the first step. The rest will follow.

Doing the right thing
is usually the easiest.

What you have achieved
today, you dreamt
of yesterday. Dreams
can come true.

To become accomplished
at what you want to do,
choose something
you love doing.

TO REMOVE NEGATIVE
ENERGY FROM YOUR
SURROUNDINGS,
SMUDGE WITH SAGE

1

Take the tightly bound leaves
of sage and light the end.

2

Blow out the flames and allow
the embers to glow.

3

Use the smoke produced to waft
through the air around you.

4

Repeat 'the air is clear' out loud,
three times. Be sure to dowse the
burning embers after you have
completed this ritual.

It may sound like a cliché, but today is truly the first day of the rest of your life.

In an uncertain world,
a daily routine can help
you feel grounded.

Don't feed the wolf that
stalks your peace of mind.
Calmly bid it leave.

The answer lies not in trying
harder, but in trying differently.

Make a list of all your
progress and achievements,
from the little to the large,
and give each a gold star.
Pin it to your wall or keep
it in your purse.

Do not let a busy diary
rule your life: factoring
in downtime is essential.

Your feelings are your emotions in action: use them to your best advantage.

Take responsibility for your own cup and make sure it's always half full and not half empty.

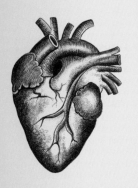

Choose a one-syllable word
on which to focus your
attention: tree, space, love,
book, cup, song. Start by
seeking its simple meaning
and see what wisdom
it inspires in you.

Sometimes the elephant
in the room is you.

Idleness can free your mind
and free your thoughts.

On each new moon, take
a few moments to consider the
possibilities of new beginnings
over the next lunar cycle. Make
a commitment to your best self
to embrace these.

There is magic in the
number three, look out for
it in your daily life.

The quality of your
relationships is directly related
to the quality
of your life.

There is no rule that says
you have to be perfect.

Transform the ghosts
of your past into the
ancestors of your future.

Your idea is a seed sown.
Your hard work will nourish it
to fruition.

Stop spending your precious mental energy on avoiding what needs to be done: just do it.

Don't wish for the moon
when you have the stars.

There's no time limit on success. Start now to make your dreams a reality.

TWO SIGNS YOU ARE ON TARGET

1

It feels right.

2

The end is in sight.

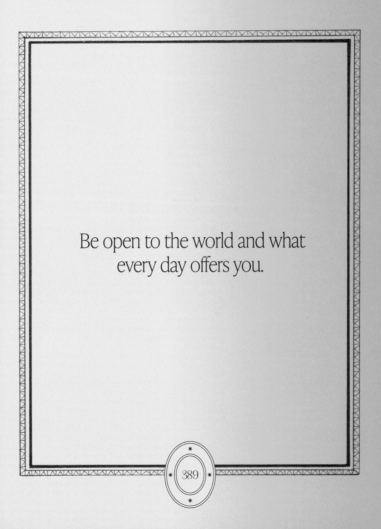

Be open to the world and what
every day offers you.

What is important isn't
always visible to the eye:
only with your heart can
you see clearly.

Let go of those things that
no longer serve you and cherish
those that do.

Avoid those people who aggravate and vex you, but welcome those who challenge and support you.

Don't normalise crazy-busy
behaviour. Chaos
is just a distraction from
what really matters.

Remember that daily rest is the foundation on which you build your power.

An easy life doesn't always yield success. Out of struggle and adversity comes great strength of character.

Share your joys as well
as your troubles.

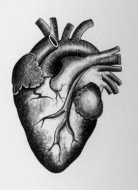

WHEN INSPIRATION
ESCAPES YOU,
TRY THE FOLLOWING

1

Take a walk.

2

See a friend.

3

Contemplate the view.

Celebrate your friends'
successes and they will
welcome yours.

A full moon is a full stop. An end to a cycle. Close the door on what did not work for you and start again on something new.

Make authenticity
and integrity your
touchstones, they will
support you well.

To burnish the love
in your heart, keep
a piece of rose quartz
crystal nearby.

Do not fear intimacy.
We come closer
to knowing ourselves
when we allow
ourselves to become
close to others.

If you are looking
for a sign, then start
with what you know.

When patterns in your life
keep repeating, learn their
lesson and move on.

Ensure that you
are feeding your body
and mind with good
ingredients.

Your soulmate is your
needs recognised.

Look for the magic
in everyday life. It's often where
you least expect it.

Change will always be an
aspect of life: embrace it.

When you doubt your ability to go on, remember that the universe has your back and wants you to succeed.

Look for the small, still
centre of calm
at the heart of every
hurricane.

Life is never perfect
and that's its beauty.

Set boundaries.
Claim your space and
leave others to theirs.

Give others the
encouragement you
would like to receive and
the path will open.

First impressions aren't
everything but they're
a good start. Make
yours count.

Risk spontaneity.
Risk curiosity.
Then see what doors
open for you.

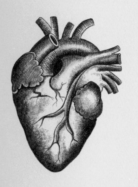

Be the type of person
you'd most like to meet.

WHEN PREPARING
FOR A BIG EVENT,
REMEMBER THESE
THREE THINGS

1
Prepare.

2
Practise.

3
Smile.

Never kill a spider.
Instead, ask for the
blessing of the Greek
goddess Arachne and
leave it in peace.

If the answer isn't clear today,
try again tomorrow.

Slow down. It doesn't always have to be done in a hurry.

A small bunch of lavender,
lemon balm and rosemary in
a vase nearby will help ward
off negative thoughts.

IMPROVE YOUR INTUITION WITH THIS MEDITATION

1

Sit quietly alone.

2

Visualise something
of meaning to you.

3

Imagine it surrounded
with white light.

4

Look out for its appearance within
the next 24 hours.

Express pleasure in the joy
already in your life and you
will attract more.

The cure for boredom
is curiosity. Explore your
world, starting with what's
on your doorstep.

You may not be able to change
the start of something, but
you have the power to choose
how it will continue.

We live life in the
present. Embrace this
and it will set you free.

Your first draft is never your
last draft, it is a step on the
way to something complete.

To embrace your creativity, you
have to have the courage to let
go of certainty.

When feeling out of sorts,
reconnect your body and brain
by sorting the laundry or
tidying your desk.

It's only after the event that
you will know how good your
timing was.

If the rules don't fit,
make your own.

Do you want to be right,
or happy? Sometimes
it pays to keep quiet.

Make a commitment
to yourself to find the space
for your dreams.

The first evening star
you see is usually Venus, the
planet of love.
Wish on it every time.

Recognise that luck often
plays a part in our progress
and make the most of it.

The only thing stopping
you is the voice in your
head.

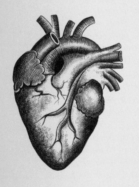

There is a magic in paying it forwards: no good deed goes unrewarded.

Sometimes you
have to move the
goalposts if you
want to score.

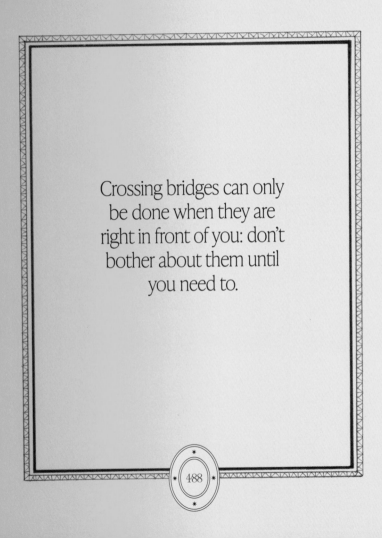

Crossing bridges can only
be done when they are
right in front of you: don't
bother about them until
you need to.

If it no longer serves your
purpose, let it go.

In the cycle of life,
regeneration occurs many
times. You can reinvent
yourself and prosper.

Align your aims to your
values to increase your
chance of success.

Do not attach too
much importance to what
others say; the only true
voice is yours.

Trusting the divine is all
about trusting yourself.

Resilience comes from
having the courage to
expose yourself to life.
It will serve you well.

Check in with the balance
of your life. Does it feel
good? If not, ask yourself
for what you need and the
universe will answer.

Sow the seeds of your success
every day. Repeat
to yourself: I am worth it.

Respect the time it takes
to heal. It will happen.

Remind your younger self that all will be well. You have the power to make it so.

ACKNOWLEDGEMENTS

First and foremost, thanks are due to my inspirational and creative publisher Kate Pollard, who is always willing to go the extra mile to produce books of substance and beauty. And to the illustrator, Lucy Pollard, and design team at Evi O. Studio for creating such a gorgeous book.

Thanks are also due to my teachers, past and present, who inspired me on my journey as an esoteric practitioner, enabling me to develop my own skills and talents. And to my Romany grandmother who provided insights to a world beyond our immediate reality, and access to it.

Finally, to my family on this journey we call life, thank you for your support and love.

ABOUT THE AUTHOR

Gaia Elliot is a green witch based in London. She loves tending to her garden and being surrounded by the abundance of nature, which feeds into her spell-casting and magic-making. Gaia believes that anyone can harness their inner power by tapping into their intuition. She has a strong interest in tarot, the power of the moon and psychology.

Gaia's spiritual journey started when she was a young woman, and she loves nothing more than helping other people to start or continue their own. This is her first book.

Published in 2024 by Hardie Grant Books,
an imprint of Hardie Grant Publishing

Hardie Grant Books (London)
5th & 6th Floors
52–54 Southwark Street
London SE1 1UN

Hardie Grant Books (Melbourne)
Building 1, 658 Church Street
Richmond, Victoria 3121

hardiegrantbooks.com

British Library Cataloguing-in-Publication Data.
A catalogue record for this book is available from the British Library.

The Book of Answers
ISBN: 978-178488-950-0

10 9 8 7 6 5 4 3 2 1

Publishing Director: Kate Pollard
Copy Editor: Hannah Boursnell
Design: Evi-O. Studio | Katherine Zhang, Susan Le
Illustrator: Lucy Pollard
Production Controller: Gary Hayes

Colour reproduction by p2d
Printed and bound in China by Leo Paper Products Ltd.